KIDS
IN TROUBLE

OTHER BOOKS BY THE AUTHOR

Wilderness Road

and

CO-AUTHOR WITH LYNN LOUGHMILLER

Camping and Christian Growth

Let's Go Camping

Big Thicket Legacy

Kids In Trouble

an adventure in education

Campbell Loughmiller

Wildwood Books
Post Office Box 7263
Tyler, Texas 75711

Printed in USA

Dedicated to my
daughter and son

Camelia and Grover

"Treat people as if they were what they ought to be and you help them become what they are capable of being."

—*Goethe*

KIDS
IN TROUBLE

CONTENTS

11

FOREWORD

Campbell Loughmiller's camp was unlike any I had ever seen. Accustomed as I was to the kind of summer camps we all know—with cottages, lodges, tennis courts, baseball diamonds, craft shops, riding stables and all the rest— his camp seemed strangely empty at first. Where exactly, *was* this camp?

All we saw after the winding drive in from the highway was a headquarters building, a shower house, and a rustic dining hall, with an attached supply room. That was all that looked familiar. There were no children to be seen or heard so Loughmiller and I started off down the trail to find the boys.

A walk in the woods with Loughmiller is never a simple affair, nor a hasty one. We walked purposefully but unhurriedly down a well-kept trail for a quarter-mile or so towards the nearest group, while he told me about the camp.

His account was a seamless blend of camp history, with gentle anecdotes about particular boys and what they made of their camp experience. As we passed a rotting log not far from the edge of the trail, he explained how it would be good for an hour's discussion on time and its measurement, on history, on ecological systems, on the inter-relationship between people and their environment.

We soon reached the campsite, unimpressive by usual standards: a cluster of hogans of ingenious designs made from saplings, canvas and transluscent plastic sheeting.

There were still no children to be seen, but voices in lively debate came from the largest hogan, which I learned serves as a combination dining room and general meeting place. As we entered, ten boys and two young men were gathered around a sturdy, hand-hewn table, examining highway maps of Texas and Mexico. At first no one paid any attention to us, so engrossing was the discussion. The topic was public health—specifically, a state's right to require vaccination.

The boys were, I learned, in their sixth week of planning a trip by camp bus through South Texas and into Mexico. Although such treks are exceptions, not the rule at the camp, they are invaluable, for they become centers around which the boys gain instruction, then first-hand experience in such diverse areas as arithmetic, composition, American history, government, even art and music; and most of all, in responsible planning.

At this camp there is no school as such, for learning goes on all the time.

The boys are delighted with visitors, and proudly took us to see what they had made of their camp: the kitchen with an oil drum-and-baked-mud oven; their sleeping hogans, each with hard-packed clay floor, and wood piled by the stove against the winter's night; the pow-wow area, a ring of logs around a small campfire, a place for serious discussions each night; a nearby salt lick surrounded by smoothly-raked sand to reveal the tracks of night visitors.

After a shorter visit than I might have liked, we moved on to the next campsite, a quarter of a mile removed.

There are five campsites in all, each of distinctive design and in the process of being built, modified or extended. Each camp has ten boys and two counselors, in some stage of an enterprise that captures their interest and sustains purpose.

Watching the boys at work it is hard to realize that they are children in deep trouble, with themselves and with society. They were first failed by family, school, neighborhood, church, and then they were rejected as anti-social, delinquent, or emotionally disturbed—labels given children by adults to legitimize their exclusion from normal opportunities to grow up well. They get a second chance at camp, and most of them make good of it.

Why does camp work when other social institutions have failed these boys so profoundly? There is no magic in the woods; done poorly, camping can be a disaster for children and adults alike.

But camp can simplify things, remove kids from school and other settings where defeat and despair have become their constant companions. Camp can give these children new opportunities to learn about themselves and others, about skills they will need to manage in this world. The woods simply provide a congenial setting for adults and young people to work together, guided by principles of living that have been worked out over thirty years in these camps.

The principles themselves seem—indeed are—simple enough: that young people have a tremendous desire to learn and to do well; that their feelings are intrinsically valid and quite as important as their thinking; that destructive and self-defeating behaviour must be faced; that young people can help each other sort things out and arrive at good choices; that the world is rich in things to learn; that life is to be savored at each moment; and that decent, caring adults are absolutely essential in the lives of children, if those children are to grow up strong in body, quick of mind, generous in spirit.

And the principles developed in this pioneering camp in rural East Texas, and now extended to more than thirty other programs for boys and girls across the United States, are every bit as valid for parents, teachers, indeed all adults upon whom children are dependent for help in growing up.

But it is better to let Campbell Loughmiller tell what such principles mean in working with kids in trouble, as he does in this remarkable book.

—Nicholas Hobbs, Ph.D.
Institute for Public Policy Studies
Center for the Study of Families
and Children
Vanberbilt University

PREFACE

For twenty years I directed a program for emotionally handicapped and delinquent boys, sponsored by the Salesmanship Club of Dallas. Since that time—for the last twelve years—I have served as consultant to the program, and to more than twenty others modelled along the same lines or using the same basic philosophy. These programs are in Education, Corrections, and Mental Health.

The overview this experience has afforded prompts this effort to emphasize and underscore the concepts and practices we have found most helpful, the basic aspects of our work which account for its 85% success rate with seriously disturbed boys and girls who require extended help outside the home and community. In some instances I have tried to illuminate these concepts with examples from actual experience.

In discussing the various components of the program separately—as in Education, Groupwork, or Counselor Training—I have found it impossible to avoid a degree of repetition in emphasizing considerations common to each. I felt this would be more helpful than distracting, as they are vitally inter-related.

Working with youth in trouble focuses our attention more and more on prevention. The concepts and methods discussed here are equally effective in working with kids in trouble or those considered to be normal. They are effective in the home, in the classroom, or any place where people are meaningfully related.

I have referred to boys in the text because the methods and ideas discussed were tested in working with delinquent and emotionally handicapped boys in a camp setting. However, they have proved just as effective at the girls' camp which the Salesmanship Club started more than two years ago.

In 1966 I presented a narrative account of our program in a book titled *Wilderness Road*. The ideas presented here are an extension of—not a variation from—those presented earlier. This work is written primarily for persons directly involved in working with youth: parents, teachers, counselors, and those in the fields of corrections or mental health.

—Campbell Loughmiller

October, 1978

ACKNOWLEDGEMENTS

I wish to express my appreciation to Dr. Nicholas P. Hobbs and to John D. MacInnes for reading the manuscript and making many helpful suggestions; and to Roger J. Seymour and my wife, Lynn, for their valuable editorial help in the preparation of the manuscript in its final form.

I am also grateful to Reynold Carlson, Edward L. Schlingman, Melvin Moody, Ima Jean Kidd, Dr. Vincent Cyphers, Dr. George Donaldson, and Dr. Maryhelen Vannier for reviewing the manuscript and giving me their reactions to the material.

Finally, I wish to acknowledge the interest and support of the many members of the Salesmanship Club of Dallas whose continuing devotion to boys and girls who need help has been an inspiration to all of us.

AN OVERVIEW OF THE PROGRAM

I believe every boy wants to grow up in a wholesome, mature way, but needs help with difficulties he does not know how to handle. He does not need motivation; he needs hope and help. We help him at whatever point he has difficulty. We do exactly the same thing with new counselors who have difficulty doing their job. With them we call it staff training. With campers, it is called therapy; but it is all the same thing, and it is all education.

We believe that every boy sent to us has enough resources to assume responsibility for himself and lead a satisfactory life, and we fully expect him to do it. One of our main responsibilities is to provide the opportunity, the environment, where his strengths can be discovered and his abilities can find expression. The boys we get have not had this opportunity. They come to camp from age eight to sixteen because they have been unable to function ade-

21

quately at school, at home, or in the community. They are moderately to severly disturbed. All of them are failures in school, many are in conflict with the law, and others have given up and have withdrawn from active participation in anything. All kinds of boys come—aggressive, delinquent, neurotic, schizophrenic; with brain damage, asthma, epilepsy, dyslexia and so on; but as we see it, they are not *sick* and we are not *therapists.*

They enter school and face tasks for which they are not ready, and get bogged down in difficulties that cause us to label them as "slow learners," "retarded," or "exceptional"; and we give them the works: we test them, we analyze them, we evaluate them, we label them. We employ a complex professional vocabulary which mystifies the layman, but which is inexact and means different things to different people.

We see more difficulties than opportunities, and thus begins the long cycle of frustration for the boy and the teacher. We provide a whole raft of specialists for remedial help and psychiatric treatment for boys who are not failures in themselves, but failures only in the "straight jacket" we put them in. In the process, we create a distaste for the classroom.

If a child does not succeed in school it is because he does not want to learn what we try to teach him, at the time we try to teach it, or in the way we go about it. All these variables are within our capacity to manage.

Boys reveal their problems in specific areas and we help them in concrete ways. Normally they return home at the end of their stay—sixteen to eighteen months average—and function satisfactorily at their age-grade level in school. In the relatively few instances where this has not happened, we regard it as our failure more than the boy's.

The setting

We are in the outdoors—not a wilderness setting, but at least a natural area, sufficiently removed to avoid the distractions of what we commonly call civilization. We could operate in a West Texas canyon, an East Texas forest, a Mid-West prairie, or any other environment as long as it affords the isolation required; and even this is a relative factor.

Minimum permanent facilities are provided: kitchen-dining room, bath house, warehouse and office. Boys and their leaders construct and maintain their own shelters, latrines, camp cooking-eating facilities, tool racks, wash area, garbage disposal facilities, and such other things as they require. About two-thirds of their meals are eaten in the central dining room, the others at their own small campsite.

Under supervision of their counselors, they lay out and maintain their trails, construct the water lines from the well to their campsites and do all those things necessary for safe and responsible living. Since their shelters are constructed of canvas stretched over a frame made of saplings, they require repair and replacement from time to time, and must be winterized for comfort in cold weather. Hillside trails require upkeep to prevent erosion, and woodcutting for cooking is a year-round necessity. These things provide the core of the program, the most meaningful experiences boys encounter at camp.

Here we are friends and partners in the enterprise of meeting life requirements. A boy discovers many abilities not recognized in the narrower setting of the classroom, and many opportunities are provided for him to succeed in

23

ways important to the group. Recognition is given in an obvious, if non-verbal way.

We think of this setting as offering the richest possible environment for learning. We have limitless opportunities to enlist the interest and curiosity of a boy. We not only provide the opportunity, we create the necessity for him to learn; but it is a necessity he recognizes out of his own interest, not one arbitrarily imposed. I have often thought that if, in all the world, I could choose a place to take a group of boys to have fun, to experiment, to learn, to grow toward maturity, I could think of no better place than camp.

Therapy or education, viewed here as the same thing, lies in the specific utilization of professional techniques. It does not just happen. Getting boys into the outdoors may provide a favorable setting, but it does not guarantee results. There is no magic in a camp unless we put it there.

In the simple environment of a camp, it is difficult for an inexperienced person to see the vitality of a boy's experience as it relates to his recovery from serious emotional problems for which—in many cases—he has been treated for months or years before coming. It looks so simple. It is difficult for the casual visitor to see much difference between this program and that of a group on a weekend outing; and people trained in a one-to-one approach, as I was, cannot readily assess the strength of the program. Only on the basis of actual experience in it can it be evaluated effectively. An examination of the various concepts upon which the program rests yields only a partial picture. The concepts themselves are not new or complex, but the manner in which they are inter-related in a life-wide experience gives them a cumulative value not apparent from their separate analysis.

Service provided through counselors

Traditionally we have felt that boys such as we serve required the team approach: psychiatrist, psychologist, social worker. I felt this way, too, when our program was started, and it was only on the basis of experience that my point of view changed.

Actually we have no specialists: no psychologist, no psychiatrist, no water-front man, no special teachers. Our services are channeled as fully as possible through the two counselors in charge of each group. This requires that we provide continuous on-the-job training of counselors, because three separate disciplines have their confluence in the daily life of the group: social work, education and camping. As one trained in each of these, I can say that ninety percent of all I ever learned in all three disciplines is applied daily in the life of a group that is operating well. This is achieved through attitudes and procedures that insure the best possible mental health.

In formulating the program over the years, we have had the helpful advice and consultation of persons from all of these fields, and others, and have adapted their many contributions in such a way that they find expression in daily living. If I dwell on this point a bit, it is only to say that we did not just stumble into this posture, but developed it out of continuous staff evaluation of our own experience, with the assistance of many professional resources within the community, and periodic evaluations by persons from outside.

At camp, though, these concepts are applied successfully by persons with no specialization whatever, and with varying degrees of college training. We are not therapists treating boys with an illness; we are friends helping boys with problems—problems that manifest

25

themselves in ways that are obvious to everyone in the group. This involves skill in human relations which can be applied almost anywhere by persons whose only specialization is achieved on the job. This is indeed considerable and consists mainly in implementing attitudes and techniques common in theory but scarce in practice.

Problems solved by the group

Any trouble the boy has, any difficulties he encounters, are dealt with in the context in which they arise. All members of the group are familiar with the circumstances, all are affected, and all have an interest in the solution. It would be easy enough for a counselor to call a boy aside and come to an understanding, but this does not help. The reality of it is in the group where every member is involved. That is where it counts.

Only when a boy's peers and his leaders—the group—bring a problem to a satisfactory conclusion does it achieve its full meaning, not only to the boy in trouble, but to all of them. It is in the repeated use of this process that a boy develops the greatest insight into his own behavior. With the helpful participation of his peers he is usually able to overcome the difficulties that brought him to camp; but what is equally important, he acquires a frame of reference, a set of values, a basic attitude, a problem-solving technique, a tool, a method that will serve him well throughout his life.

It is necessary to remember that the groups are semi-autonomous, with enough flexibility to meet any situation or difficulty whenever they encounter it. When a problem arises they solve it on the spot. Nothing supersedes it in importance. They are never too rushed to handle any situation as it arises. We are just living together, not carrying out a "program," and this allows us the opportunity to put first things first. To us this means that we do not move ahead on anything until our feelings have been cleared. We do not move until we can move as friends.

The process used in dealing with all problems is essentially the same. Most problems arise—directly or indirectly—from a boy's feelings about himself or others. The most common observation that could be made of all boys who come to us is that they have no confidence in themselves, no positive self-image, no trust in adults; and this has almost invariably resulted in scholastic failure. The method works equally well for "normal" boys or the seriously handicapped—the severly withdrawn, or the aggressive, hostile boys whose bizarre behavior makes the headlines. It simply requires more time in some cases.

Factors in grouping

It has been suggested that we determine which "type" of boy we are able to help best, and govern our intake accordingly. If, for instance, we could help a social delinquent in less time than boys with other difficulties, we could profitably confine our intake to this type of boy. On the surface this seems like a good suggestion but in practice it does not work out that way.

In the first place, there are too many variables to make an accurate judgment about the relative value of the program for boys with different kinds of problems: the support he gets from his family, the extent and duration of his difficulties, whether he lives with his family or in a foster home, his neighborhood, his native capacities, and many other factors that are difficult to measure.

At camp, too, his progress is influenced by the skill of his counselors, the stability of the group to which he is assigned, staff turn-over, and other things. But even if all these factors could be accurately assessed, it would be a mistake to constitute a group of boys with similar problems. Homogeneous grouping, to the extent it can be achieved, does not provide the variety of skills, attitudes, interests, and stimulation that are so vital to a boy's growth. If it were possible to have a group with similar problems, the growth of all the members, and in all areas, would be sharply reduced. Diversity promotes group achievement as well as the maximum growth of individual members.

There are ten boys in a group and all of them are involved in every decision that is made affecting their life. The requirements of living constitute what we generally call "program": food, shelter, and recreation. The group decides what needs to be done and organizes to do it: the number and type of shelters they will need, the trips they will take, and hundreds of other things, big and little, that make up the requirements of pleasant living; but more important, they know the reason behind every plan they make.

The group process is used all the time. It is a way of life, not just a tool employed occasionally as "therapy." It is a consciously-guided group discussion used in setting goals, determining procedures, evaluating performance, solving a problem or establishing norms of behavior.

The same two counselors work with the group continuously. They alternate in taking time off, but on trips away from camp both are on duty. This makes it possible to undertake trips of two to four weeks or longer by bus, raft, or canoe with maximum flexibility. It also facilitates the identification of boys with their leaders. We find a boy

makes little progress until he feels secure in the friendship
of at least one adult—one he can trust implicitly.

Groupwork must be taught on the job, as counselors
do not have this skill when they begin. It is the primary
method we employ, the one we find most effective.

Group values

The values that are important in the life of the group
emerge from the way they live, the decisions they make,
and how they make them, rather than from discussions of
hypothetical situations. These values are treated more
directly at religious services Sunday morning and at
Vespers on Wednesday; but these, too, are handled by the
groups and are consonant with the attitudes they exhibit
throughout the week.

The groups are continuous. Not more than two boys
leave a group during any month, which means no more
than two new ones are added. In this way, the equilibrium
of the group is not seriously affected and we are able to
preserve the peer culture—the accumulation of attitudes
and values held by the group, a nucleus of positive leadership without which our work would be complicated
beyond words.

These values have been hammered out of the daily experience of the group, and are held by the members as
their own. Although they may coincide with those of the
counselors, they are not acquired by adoption. Their effectiveness has been demonstrated in their own experience.

From the standpoint of our work, the counselor is the
most important person in the life of a boy while he is at
camp. His position is primary and we reinforce it in every
way possible. Educational opportunities are simply

unlimited at camp, and counselor training is in large part
an effort to bring about increased awareness of these opportunities and the ways of using them most effectively.
He is the group leader because he has more experience and
maturity. He protects the timid from the bully and sees
that no one is made a scapegoat. He sets limits if, for some
reason, the group is temporarily unable to do so. He
works consciously to develop attitudes that create a
healthy group climate. He is a friend, a helper, a resource
person.

If the counselor's motivation is sound when he first
comes to work, it is inevitably deepened by his involvement with the boys. He cannot do the job half-heartedly;
he will either invest himself or get out. He cannot escape
the realization that his own efforts will be a major factor
in shaping the life of the boys in his group. He comes to
understand and appreciate their struggle for social survival, their search for a friend:

> "One person like no other I have seen
> Who knows that deep inside my profane life
> There burns a spark of goodness
> Waiting for a breath of love
> To fan it into flame."*

Dr. Karl Menninger, speaking of psychiatrists, said
that, "What he *is* has more effect on a patient than
anything he *does.*" I think it is equally true of counselors.

Elements of education and discipline

Ego growth is anchored in the mastery of a wide range
of minute, common experiences, physical and social. Our

---

*Author Unknown

efforts in a boy's behalf, therefore, must aim at helping him learn to do the usual—not the unusual—things: build a fire, saw a log; cook a meal, dig a post hole; make his bed, lash a table; write a letter, bait a hook; sing a song, paddle a canoe; stalk an animal, make a friend. When he learns to do the things in keeping with his age level, the things most boys his age can do—when he is at par for his age, so to speak—he is no longer a problem. This includes physical, social and academic skills. There are things we can teach and the boy can learn.

It was a surprise to me that learning, even to a boy who has never experienced success in school, is one of the most satisfying things in his life. Deprive him of the opportunity and he will raise more hell than we can handle—and this from boys who could not be contained in a classroom! One has to wonder how it happens: teachers want to teach, and kids want to learn, and yet, for many, school has become a battleground. How in the world do we manage it?

There is no short, simple answer, but of one thing I feel sure—a boy wants to learn and, if he can see any hope whatever of success, he will work hard to achieve it. What he learns must be related to his own interests in terms that he can understand and accept, an essential factor in all effective learning.

Recently I was in a school principal's office when he was interviewing a prospective teacher. One of his first questions was, "Can you handle discipline?" I guess we all know what he meant. It is a primary problem with us. It is perhaps a new counselor's first concern, but we could never achieve discipline in arbitrary or authoritative ways. In an environment where there is no punishment, where a boy can run off when he chooses, our only hope of discipline is through satisfying experiences responsibly undertaken. We have to make sense to the boys.

Structure comes from group goals in meeting life requirements. Discipline comes from group organization to accomplish them, on the basis of concrete, specific plans. Good plans, understood by each member, are the procedural means of achieving the maximum satisfaction from any undertaking. This gives meaning to each step in the process, the relationship of the part to the whole. This simple process contains three interdependent ingredients—discipline, education and democracy—all of which reinforce each other and contribute to the same end—responsible living.

Occasionally a new counselor prefers an assignment with the smaller boys—eight to ten years old. He thinks he would feel more secure, could control them better. Actually, this is not true. No two counselors on earth could "control" them but, through sound groupwork process, discipline can be achieved through the participation of the members themselves. If a counselor operates with small boys in a way he cannot use with boys as large as he is, or larger, it is not a sound procedure anyway. The process is the same and it will work with any age group.

Role of the parent

A boy's goals and the revisions that are made from time to time form the basis of our work with him while he is at camp. His parents are fully involved in the intake process and participate in the regular evaluations of his progress each three months. Historically, they have shown a willingness to make necessary changes in the management of the boy based on new insights or changing circumstances. Parents, like the boys, tend to live up to our expectations or down to our doubts.

We have found these evaluation conferences most effective, not only in overcoming a boy's problems at camp, but in promoting better parent-child relationships—a suitable atmosphere for his continued growth at home. The full involvement of parents throughout a boy's stay is the best insurance we have found against post-camp regression.

Let me say here what has been implied already: the program is effective. Boys with almost every kind and degree of difficulty have returned home to function satisfactorily. A two-year research project by Dr. Don McNeil and associates, of the University of Texas, shows that eighty-five percent of the boys who leave camp are able to lead responsible and successful lives. The study covered a twenty-year period.

To summarize: these results are achieved by working with disturbed youth in the outdoors in small, primary groups, getting their education through life experiences determined largely by necessity. They are guided by a groupwork process employed continuously by the same two leaders, which facilitates identification and provides flexibility in programming. Discipline is achieved through the pursuit of individual and group goals on the basis of specific plans made by the group and understood by each member. The goals are both immediate and long range. In the daily evaluation of their performance in reaching these goals—physical or social—values, attitudes, and norms of behavior are developed, a group culture that becomes a major influence in shaping the growth of all members.

EDUCATION

Conditions necessary for growth

We believe that every person—every living organism in fact—has a tendency to grow and mature and develop its potential. The seeds of a desert flower may lie on the ground for three years, but with a good rain they will sprout and grow and reproduce. And if you plant an acorn in a favorable spot with enough rainfall and sunlight, it will make a good oak.

A human being is the same way. The natural, inherent tendency of the organism is to grow and mature and, in the case of kids, to be wholesome and accepted. But they get derailed by difficulties they do not know how to manage and get bogged down in conflict at home, or elsewhere, through an effort on their part to compensate for something they needed but did not get.

The reason I believe this is because we have had some of the worst stinkers in the world, with every sort of disability, and after working with them an average of eighteen months, they turn out to be persons one would like to have as a next door neighbor.

The psychological conditions, the emotional climate, that we try to maintain at camp are not just something a person might try to achieve in a "therapy session," but the environment that characterizes our interpersonal relationships throughout the day. It is a way of life. These conditions are conducive to growth and can be applied, to one degree or another, in all our relationships. They are perhaps easier to develop and maintain in small, primary groups, but are equally valid anywhere.

Dr. Charles Truax researched many disciplines of psychotherapy and found that the ingredients of successful results in all cases were the same:

1. The helper must see himself as a person of dignity and worth; he must be honest, genuine, real, a person of confidence and freedom.
2. He must have a positive regard for the person he is trying to help with no conditions whatever.
3. He must have the ability to enter into another person's life through empathy and understanding and to feel as *he* feels, to put himself in *his* place.

Carl Rogers lists the same three conditions for helping, with only slightly different wording.

For thirty years we have tried to make sure that these conditions exist as fully as possible. It is our greatest single concern. If we are successful, it is almost certain that every boy will have the freedom to examine his own feelings and attitudes honestly and to make appropriate changes. In this effort, we agree with the comment made by Dr. James

F. Berwald, Medical Director, Childrens Aid Society, Cleveland, Ohio: "Just as in medicine, no therapist cures anyone but only removes that which blocks the innate curative forces within the individual; and those curative forces need an environment in which the accent is not on treatment but on controls, discipline, standards and protection, in an atmosphere of understanding and affection."

How we help

Personality changes are not so much the result of something that is taught as they are of a relationship that is established. In the small group a boy comes to feel secure and free. He does not have to pretend; he can simply be himself. His resources are liberated; the atmosphere is conducive to the discovery and expression of his native tendencies and abilities. He comes to see himself for what he is, to measure himself against others, to achieve his own identity. He experiences the feeling of being needed, of engaging in a cause greater than himself, and this increases his sense of worth and self-respect. He acquires hope.

It is generally agreed by those who help people that basic improvement in any part of the personality is contingent on the health of the "whole" person. We help the "whole self," but we do it in specific ways. Although we are teaching specific things, as in building a fire, it will not be meaningful to the boy unless we teach with love and concern, unless we are building a relationship, too. A successful job at anything—cooking, camp building, trail-logging, or whatever—builds confidence; and it is especially effective if it has social significance through its contribution to the group.

Behavior must be faced

We cannot help a boy through a soft approach or sentimental indulgence. We deal with reality. To approach a boy's negative behavior with deference is to show a lack of confidence in his ability to deal with it responsibly; to excuse him would mean that we think he is too weak to do anything about it. If a boy in the group turns to violence, we restrain him; if he pretends inability, his excuse is not accepted; if he throws a tantrum, it is handled by the group to a satisfactory conclusion.

He cannot just blow his stack and leave; he must face up to his behavior.

There is a tendency on the part of some boys to excuse themselves because of what has happened to them in the past. This is self-defeating because a boy will never grow so long as he is allowed to lean on excuses. No matter what kind of sordid past be has had, no matter how well we understand and appreciate the circumstances that brought him to his present situation, we cannot let this relieve him of responsibility for his behavior now. We can provide a favorable environment but he is the only one who can do anything about it.

I remember an instance when a boy was involved in a discussion with his group about a problem he had created, and commented, "I've had five fathers." Almost instantly one of the boys said, "I don't care if you've had ten; that doesn't help you out of this situation." So no matter what a boy's past has been, he is held fully responsible for his present behavior; for, regardless of how his difficulties accrue, he is the only one who is able to deal with them now.

Boys assume responsibility at intake

The boy's responsibility is emphasized at intake. He must recognize his difficulties and assume responsibility for overcoming them. He comes to camp for a purpose. He does not come to have fun; he does not come to avoid school; he does not come just to get out of an unpleasant situation at home. He comes to solve a problem, a problem that gets him into difficulties which he recognizes and is able to describe.

It is undoubtedly true that the boy does look forward to having fun at camp, as he should, and that he will escape some of the tensions that he may be experiencing at home—and we work hard to see that he does; but we never paint a rosy picture of the fun he will have, the canoe trips he will make, or other romantic aspects of camp life.

Two negative results flow from this approach. First, all the boy has to do is sit back and shout his disappointment when things do not work as we painted them; and second, it does not emphasize his obligation in coming. Moreover, even if the boy came to have fun, he will not find it through irresponsible behavior. He might experience excitement now and then, but nothing positive and satisfying. Fun and satisfaction come from responsible living and this becomes self-evident to every boy in the group.

If there is any word we use more than another it is the word "responsible." We do not describe a boy's behavior as good or bad, but as responsible or irresponsible, appropriate or inappropriate, effective or ineffective.

Education involves emotions as well as intellect

In reflecting on our work with boys we find nothing that is not educational in nature. It involves education of the emotions as well as the intellect—two parts of the same process. For centuries—from the time of Socrates until fairly recently—this was the acknowledged goal of education.

Douglas Heath says, "We no longer strive to develop human excellence—but only intellectual excellence. Students play it cool—distrusting spontaneity, rejecting tenderness, affection, sentiment, weakness, serious involvement. Coolness produces emotional bankruptcy and boredom."

Dr. Bruno Bettelheim, speaking of the classroom, says, "If team work is there, we can afford to put the awkward among the skillful and, as likely as not, all will succeed. Putting the gifted children in a class by themselves removes the need for them to be helpful and is apt to lead to an over-evaluation of the intellect at the expense of human values. What is surely lacking is the education of the emotions which permits people to live at peace with themselves and others, to develop a concern for others, compassion, or a sense of service."

It has been suggested by serious students of education that every child should have two teachers in the classroom—one to educate him scholastically and one to educate him for society. We do not believe this. We believe one good teacher can do both; and further, that if a teacher cannot do both, he cannot do either. We do not need a mental health worker in the classroom, whether social worker, psychologist, or special health educator, provided we have a competent teacher. If a teacher cannot induce the necessary mental health climate, he cannot teach either, for they are inseparable. Neither do we need "crisis" teachers. This is a method often employed to our detriment—patching up a bad performance in a manner that makes it even worse. We need to provide the teacher with better training.

Dr. Edward Greenwood, of the Menninger Clinic said, "Unless we bring into the classroom, into teacher training, some of the understandings of mental health, and bring Mental Health people into a closer understanding of what can be done in the classroom, we will continue to get larger school Guidance Departments and more adjunctive services, trying to repair the damage of what was misdone in the classroom in the first place."

If we regard education in the broad sense as dealing with the emotions as well as the intellect, the flimsy partition that is thought to separate these two disciplines would disappear. For social work is where the education is—there but not visible in the conventional framework.

We are friends of the boy, closely associated in a living situation that involves meaningful tasks. The boys are free to say or do what they wish, provided they take responsibility for it and face up to the group. They are doing things they like. They are involved with concrete things that have meaning right now. They are motivated. They work as a team, each one helping the other. They are not achieving status by outdoing one another, but by some unique contribution to the group. They are valued by its members for what they can contribute to the group's welfare. They do not seek independence, but interdependence. All their senses are involved in their learning. Specific things are learned in a pattern, a process, that gives meaning to them—the relation of the part to the whole. They are not rushed, not tense. They are accepted, trusted. They feel our faith in them. The whole at-

mosphere is one of friendliness, helpfulness, and cooperation.

Social Work and Education are both involved in this
process. We do not have formal conferences with the boys
very often, but dozens of times a day there are brief but
meaningful exchanges between counselor and boy. He
learns hundreds of skills, learns to think well of himself
because others do, and because he has achieved matura-
tional skills appropriate for his age. His inner resources
are liberated by the love, friendship and acceptance of his
associates, unencumbered by the crippling effects of his
former fears and anxieties. During this process, the boy
overcomes serious difficulties for which he may have been
treated by specialists over an extended period.

This is certainly not to deny or minimize the major
contributions that specialists have made to our program.
It is just the opposite. In the formulation and refinement
of the program, we have sought the help of the best people
we could find, in workshops, seminars, and consultation.
Any originality the program has is due largely to the
organizational structure through which these services are
provided.

Use of specialists

The use of specialists, however, underscores the
assumption that the boy is the problem. For instance, if
there were a psychiatrist on the staff, it would say to the
boys that they are sick, so we need a doctor. It would say
to a counselor, "You're a good fellow, have a good heart,
but we have to 'treat' these boys and we need a specialist
to deal with the illness." We believe just the opposite. The
presence of the specialist would lessen the confidence of a

counselor, make him wonder if this boy or that one needed the help of the specialist—otherwise why is he on the staff? It registers the false notion that we do not believe he is up to the job of dealing fully and successfully with the boy. It is what it says to the boy that matters most—that we see him as the problem, that we must do something *to him* to make him more normal when, as a matter of fact, we should be changing the things outside of the boy. We need to remove the roadblocks and let the boy's own resources carry him forward, for all boys want to learn. It is as natural as breathing.

Youth have the resources to succeed

We have never had a boy at camp who did not have enough resources to succeed as a person. We have occasionally had boys referred who were said to be unable to profit from instruction; yet, they are now regularly employed at unsheltered jobs, able to meet their adult responsibilities without specialized help from anyone.

A few years back Harvard University started experimenting by accepting students who had not graduated from accredited high schools, and whose entrance scores averaged 400 instead of the 600 to 700 ordinarily required. Eighty-five percent of these two hundred or more students were graduated, some with honors. This seems to indicate that no one has yet developed a test that will measure a person's drive, ambition, interest, or perseverance. The most vital qualities of a person cannot be measured.

Favorable learning conditions

Nearly all the boys referred to us are already scholastic failures with a negative conditioning to school. They cannot learn effectively when they are burdened with anxiety that results from insecurity and failure. One of our first efforts, therefore, is to help each boy achieve a secure place in his group, a feeling of acceptance and belonging. We are concerned at this point in building a relationship of friendliness and concern between the boy and his counselors and peers. When this is done, learning comes easily. He has a natural curiosity, which means he wants to learn, and we try to expand and encourage its growth.

It is a well-accepted fact that one learns more quickly and retains longer those things that have greatest meaning to him. We try, therefore, to make sure that the rewards of learning are immediate and certain for, at the outset, boys are not capable of investing much energy in deferred goals. They live in the present. They build a fire for a meal they will eat two hours later; they cut poles for a tent they will build the next day; they write an article for the camp paper about a bobcat they saw thirty minutes ago. We try to capitalize immediately on those teachable moments when interest and enthusiasm are high. No abstract learning could equal these things in interest and motivation.

All we have to do is use those occasions that are most opportune. It does not matter so much what the group is doing as how they feel toward each other as they do it. This is true in all aspects of the boy's growth, whether in the development of a better self-image, in the acquisition of new skills, or in any other aspect of his growth.

We have at camp an unexcelled opportunity to teach— almost every favorable condition known. Drs. Paul Mort and William Vincent list the following:

"1. A person learns most quickly and lastingly what has meaning for him.

2. Before the facts and skills of teaching come friendliness, security, acceptance. No one learns well when he doesn't belong, any more than a plant can grow without roots in the soil.

3. Learning is more efficient and longer lasting when conditions are real and lifelike.

4. Facts and skills are best learned when they are part of a pattern, when we learn them in relation to their use—as a part of a job, project, or enterprise.

5. Students learn better if they see with the eyes, touch with the hands, hear with the ears, heft with the muscle, as they see with the mind's eye.

6. Behavior is controlled by the emotions as well as the intellect. Far more than a place to train the mind, the school is (should be) concerned with training the emotions also."

All our work is educational in nature

We have all kinds of boys referred, diagnosed as having everything from schizophrenia to dyslexia. New labels are constantly being created to describe them, and yet eighty-five percent of the seriously disabled kids make a satisfactory recovery and are able to assume the usual responsibilities appropriate to their age. Regardless of their past difficulties, they return to school at their age-grade level. In looking at our work with a boy we find nothing that is not educational in nature, and yet the symptoms that brought him to camp disappear. The "dyslexia" is gone, his schizoid condition has vanished, he is no longer hyperkinetic, his antisocial behavior ceases, and his "learning disabilities" are overcome. Our contribution to his recovery consists primarily in providing a warm emotional climate where he feels accepted by peers and adults, where he is helped to acquire physical, social, and educational skills related to his immediate environment but applicable anywhere.

The meaning of commonplace experiences

The things a group does for its own welfare have the greatest growth potential—constructing shelters, cutting wood, cooking. They are not the most dramatic, not the most adventuresome, but the most satisfying. If a group did nothing but eat and sleep for the first two months, but did so responsibly, and exploited the learning opportunities, there could be no more meaningful experiences for building a boy's self-concept or for teaching academic skills.

For twenty years, I asked every boy who left camp what he had enjoyed most during his stay, and the only two answers I ever got were "cutting our wood" and "building our shelters." It gives a boy a feeling of security when he acquires a wide range of simple but essential skills in meeting life on its simplest terms. He may find more adventure or excitement in other experiences but nothing so meaningful as those simple physical skills that man has relied on for comfort and survival for untold centuries, and in all parts of the world.

This was pointedly emphasized to us in a short-term camping experiment (discussed later) when we took groups of eight boys directly from Dallas on a six-week trip. In order to acquire some of the skills they would need, they spent the first five days at Metzger's Lake, a secluded spot seventy miles from Dallas. There they concentrated on such things as setting up their tents, taking them down, fire building, cooking, dishwashing, use of the axe, saw and pocket knife; also safety, conservation measures, and the like. This was all they did except for a few short rambles near the camp—no swimming, fishing, or boating—just learning the things that make for smooth operation on the road.

During the trip, they had many unusual experiences: deep sea fishing in the Gulf of Mexico, climbing eight thousand foot mountains in West Texas, exploring underground caverns, a side trip to Mexico. But, at the end of an eventful six-weeks, when each boy was asked individually and separately (in the evaluation with his parents) what he liked best about the trip, eight out of eight had the same spontaneous answer: "Metzger's!"

The second trip followed the same pattern but spent the first five days near Meridian, in the cedar brakes of Central Texas, an unlikely spot for boys with the world before them. At the end of the trip, however, it was the same thing all over again, exactly. Meridian was the highlight of their trip. It was only because these were the places where they acquired more skills, achieved the greatest satisfaction in terms of personal growth.

Learning appropriate for age is important

All learning, all growth, is sequential and in programming for emotionally disturbed, insecure boys, we do not leap over broad areas of experience to pursue adventure in types of experience for which they are not ready and which, therefore, may compound the difficulty. They need to climb a hill before they climb a mountain; they need the calm waters of a lazy stream before they canoe the white waters; they learn to cut a sapling before they fell a tree. More skill is required for a person to mount the twenty-five-foot diving board and do the half-gainer, but the ability to swim when the boat capsizes gives one more security.

Generally speaking, kids want to learn to do the things most persons their age can do, things appropriate for their age. These are sometimes called developmental tasks. If a child cannot read at five, there is no problem, but if he cannot read at eight he knows something is wrong, because most other eight-year-olds are reading. He does not worry about basketball when he is still playing marbles, but he is concerned about his ability to do the things that are commonly engaged in by boys of his age.

It is, therefore, important in helping a child build a sense of security that we teach him to do the usual, not the unusual, things. He may go through life and never be able to come off the high diving board, yet that will not affect his self-confidence, for it is an optional skill pursued by those who have a special interest in aquatics. It is when he sees himself as weak or inferior in those things that are commonly within the ability of his peers that he begins to feel inadequate and insecure, and it is in these areas that our help is most effective.

Although at first we emphasize the development of a boy's self-confidence, we do not wait until this is complete to start his academic learning, for this is a vital part of the process. When a boy is seriously retarded in school, any little academic achievement he makes may be the highlight of his day. We must, therefore, have a sharp focus on a boy's needs and his strengths in order to be effective in working with him.

Teachable moments

It is sometimes easy to get caught up in a program of action and lose sight of the most important reason we are in camp. If a group is trying to finish its menus in time to go canoeing before lunch, it is easy to neglect the golden opportunity to teach. In deciding what the menu will be and whether it comes within the alloted budget, a counselor may rely on the ablest members of the group to carry the ball and neglect the opportunity to work individually with the boy who needs help the most. In fact, one of the tendencies we have to guard against most is over-scheduling, thus losing the opportunity to savor the experiences of the day, and to utilize them for individual growth.

We want to achieve an appropriate balance—"in gear" but not hurried. We should be sufficiently relaxed to exploit any opportunity—to observe the aramadillo foraging near the campsite; to watch the slow but mortal combat between a King snake and a Copperhead; the first flower that pops through the ground in the spring; the skunk that wanders indifferently through the campsite; or listen to the coyotes on their nightly quest for food.

To rush past these things is to foreclose *natural* opportunities to teach. A good counselor never stops with the simple, sensory experience of the moment, but expands the group's insight through discussion or possibly through the use of reference books. There is a little education and a little mental health in all of it.

Recently I visited the campsite of a group of eleven-twelve year-olds. One of the boys wanted to show me something immediately. An Orb spider had spun a large, beautiful web from the top of the mosquito net over his bed to the roof of the tent, and there he still sat, off to one side. The boy had not used his mosquito net for four days lest he disturb the spider. He told me what the spider did when an insect hit the web, and went out and caught an insect and threw it in the web to prove it. All the boys had learned a good deal about the spider, but it was in his tent and on his bed, and, from the way he talked, it was his spider.

A good counselor would not let this situation pass without getting from the boy a first-rate article for the camp newspaper. If the boy is unable to read or write, or spell well, what better opportunity would a counselor ever have to teach? He would involve the group in the discussion of all they had learned about the spider, to broaden and deepen their understanding, but only one boy would write the article.

If the group were building a shelter that day, one counselor could take the other nine boys and go ahead with it while the other helped the boy write the article. He would not write it for him, he would not put words in his mouth, but he would teach him at the point he needed help. No one would think this amiss or a show of favoritism for, until a counselor values a well-written article as much as building a shelter, his confused priorities will short-circuit the learning opportunities that are everywhere around him.

At the next campsite I visited, the boys were eager to show me the bird's nest that had been built in the fold of their tent. They knew how long it had taken the bird to build the nest, when she started laying her eggs, the usual incubation period; and they were pleased that the bird was unafraid, flying near them as it went to and from its nest, and laying her eggs as they passed two feet away. You have only one guess as to the bird's identity. Yes, it was a wren.

The time the boys spend watching the bird is not wasted. But here again, an experienced counselor will carry this experience much beyond what they see and hear there. (And believe it or not, as I write this, a Black-headed Grosbeak has flown to the table where I'm working, in the Davis Mountains, and is eating seed I put out less than three feet away. He shows no fear whatever. Other birds light in the limbs of the tree above and watch with envy, but do not dare come so close.) One of the boys will write an article about this experience that will provide interesting reading in the camp newspaper. In fact, any group in camp could write a most exciting book about their experiences during any given month. For teaching a wide range of academic skills it would be as interesting and valuable as any textbook they will find.

Opportunities for education are endless

It is possible, though, for an untrained counselor to miss these deeply satisfying experiences. Conscientious and well-motivated counselors may miss them simply because they are not aware of their importance, or lack the skill to exploit them.

I am reminded of an eleven year old boy who would hardly talk when he first came to camp. One of his problems was that he could not get along in school. I happened to be there when he came to camp and also when he had his first evaluation three months later. The counselors felt that he had made very good progress, his parents were pleased, and the boy, himself, seemed to agree. When the discussion ended an hour and a half later, someone said to

51

the boy, "Wayne, if this were a report card from school do you think you would be passing?" Without replying, he began to cry, and tears rolled down his cheeks. His mother asked him why he was crying and his sobbing reply was, "I can't read."

Wayne lacked neither the intelligence nor the interest to learn to read; all he needed was help. He knew that when he left camp he would return to school and face certain failure unless he could read. Wayne's inability to read did not create conflict in the group, and an inexperienced counselor can neglect the boy who does not cause overt trouble. With more training and experience, however, he learns to know the needs of each boy intimately and to use selectively the teaching opportunities that are most appropriate.

Our total effort to help a boy is a unitary process that cannot be separated into parts. We do not implement one aspect of our work, then another, and another; it is not like a layer cake that is built layer by layer, but rather like a pound cake that is of one piece. It all rises together, or it does not rise.

The opportunities for education are endless. Every physical and psychological condition favorable to the process is available many times a day—no classroom, no "teacher," no playground, no examinations, no grades, *no failures*. If every boy in camp does not achieve the educational success we should expect of him, it has implications for counselor training. No additional personnel is needed, as this would be to abdicate our first responsibility and our finest opportunity.

Integrity of the program

This brings to mind the need to protect the integrity of the program by seeing that any extension of program, anything added, is in keeping with its philosophy and organization. It is possible to make changes of seemingly minor importance which impose serious restrictions in areas of vital importance.

We hear the suggestion now and then that we hire a "teacher" to help the boys academically. No one familiar with the program could make the suggestion, for it ignores the fact that we have two "teachers" in each group with unexcelled opportunities to teach.

These boys were in school for years and it was the scene of their commonest failure. At camp we help eighty-five percent of them return to school, most of them at their age-grade level. To suggest that we return to a pattern of failure in the face of these results would seem like the highest expression of an undying faith in a system that serves most children well, but some not at all.

We have at camp a small, atypical group composed of boys who have overcome most of their problems and are ready to go home, but the home situation may make it inopportune for them to return at the moment; or, a boy without a home may be waiting for foster home placement. We do not usually have more than four or five boys in this group and they go to public school in a nearby town.

In showing some visitors through camp once we came to the eleven year old group, and it was mentioned that one of the boys was shortly to join the group that went to school. "To catch up on his school work?" a visitor asked. "No," the boy said, "we catch up on our school work out here."

What is even more important, however, is that a boy would have to be pulled out of the group for an hour or so just when they planned to cut wood on the back side of the property, or fish at the lake, or sort their laundry, or solve a problem. Flexibility in planning, so important to the group would be seriously impaired, even if only one boy were involved. It would nullify the very thing we prize most in helping a boy—freedom for the group to make plans and carry them out.

Similar suggestions could be cited, any one of which might fit admirably in a program organized around different concepts: flush toilets, organized sports, electrical outlets at the campsites, gardening, milk cows, pets, goats to clear the underbrush, hogs to kill the snakes. All these suggestions have been made by persons deeply interested in helping—but the program is based on a few inter-related concepts, and changes in any area should be made only after a knowledgable appraisal of their over-all effect. Only a person with a sensitive awareness of program priorities can do this well.

Field trips

Field trips are sometimes undertaken as an extension of the educational process at camp. They serve a good purpose if a group is sufficiently organized to undertake them responsibly. Inexperienced counselors sometimes see it as a way "to pull the group together," but if the group is not already "together," a trip will not do the job. It is like having a baby to save a marriage—it rarely works. A group that is not functioning well can make a thousand-mile trip and come back worse than when they left.

Trips are not solutions to difficilties, but opportunities

for growth. They achieve their fullest meaning when they are an extension of a sound and satisfying program at camp.

Trips have to be undertaken on the basis of careful planning of the route, the purposes, the goals, and the sort of information they expect to get from specific facilities. This, in turn, requires them to work out balanced menus within their budgetary limitations, and to assemble their supplies and equipment, all of which requires cooperation and responsibility in planning. No good purpose is served unless these conditions prevail. Seventy percent of the value of a trip is achieved before groups leave camp.

A trip gives a group a chance to integrate a wide variety of skills they have acquired as they work on a single enterprise requiring the best from each of them. They visit such places as wildlife sanctuaries, working ranches, manufacturing plants, scenic areas, anything of interest. In working out their objectives for each visit, and making necessary arrangements, the group is necessarily involved in numerous academic skills. Opportunities for learning are limited only by the imagination of the leaders.

The preparation is not done hurriedly. A successful two-week trip may require a month's preparation, but other things will be done during the month as well. Boys have neither the patience nor the emotional stamina to pursue their preparations to a quick finish and, besides, there is no need for it. As groups achieve cohesiveness and high morale, however, they can finish anything they undertake with more speed and efficiency. This is why we put primary emphasis on employing a sound group process right from the beginning, for it tends to develop both the ability and responsibility of the members.

Trips also offer various types of adventure when groups are ready for it. But it is not necessary even to leave the property for adventure. We camped for the first six years on less than two hundred acres without making a single trip; but we pressed for the opportunity to make them because of the interest and diversity they provide. A group never feels any urgency to get away from camp, however, and trips are not held out as any kind of reward. Generally, our best trips are those of three weeks duration or less, and it is rare that any group makes more than two such trips in a year. Canoe trips by river to the Gulf of Mexico, or raft trips, are necessarily longer. Shorter trips to nearby points are made more often.

Short-term tripping vs. fixed site

In an effort to serve greater numbers, the camp experimented ten years ago with a short-term camping program of a month to six weeks for boys with incipient problems. With a little orientation they boarded the bus and left. The trips involved considerable travel, as groups usually went to Colorado or New Mexico. They were designed to serve limited goals because the boys, obviously, could not come together as a group and establish serious purposes in the short time they had before leaving. They were unaccustomed to having as much influence on what they did and how they did it as the boys who lived at camp, so adult decisions came to guide them more than was anticipated.

Overall the trips served a good purpose, but failed to achieve their potential for a few obvious reasons:

1. There was no way to supervise the staff on these trips. Counselors were sometimes hired and put in the harness in a matter of days, and they simply had not acquired the skills to deal with the kind of

group problems that were certain to arise. The supervisor sometimes had to rush to the field to help settle group difficulties that counselors were unable to handle. They were unable even to begin to employ a sound groupwork process which, in itself, was a serious limitation. In our assessment of the program later we thought it was unfair to the counselors, as well as the boys, to undertake these trips without an opportunity to provide the continuing help they were certain to need.

2. Too, there was limited opportunity for meaningful, face-to-face relationships with each other due to the sheer logistics of the trip: finding a suitable place to spend the night, packing and unpacking the supplies they needed each day, finding a suitable place to build a cooking fire, getting the wood, locating the spatula that was lost on the bus, or forgetting the bottle of catsup they needed just at mealtime. Interpersonal friction would show up just when a counselor could least afford to leave the cooking, or when the other counselor was off with part of the group getting wood for the fire. These things resulted in harassed counselors and impatient kids and made it physically and psychologically difficult to settle problems constructively. When they took off next day, the boys were bright-eyed and alert for the first thirty minutes, but after that they were apt to fall asleep.

In evaluating the experience, it was decided to do the short term camping at a fixed site, and the groups were taken directly to an isolated tract of woods available to them. It was found that the requirements of daily living introduced a certain order and structure that was lacking on the road, and that the group was more closely associated in meaningful jobs throughout the day. The structure afforded more security, and there was time to settle problems as they arose. Counselors also had help, because the supervisor was available as needed.

The counselors and supervisor felt that they had more control, more influence on the group at the end of the first week than they did at the conclusion of trips as they formerly operated. They had more time to deal with the feelings of the group members, to work with them individually and to solicit group help in setting up the activities they wished to pursue. The things campers learned in their interpersonal associations were directly transferrable to their relationships to other people anywhere.

The "tripping" program had stabilized into a pattern that allowed for one week of orientation and preparation, four weeks on the road and one week for evaluations and winding up. At the fixed campsite, it was possible to camp for the entire six weeks, thus serving fifty percent more boys at the same cost.

Even more important was the decision to send only two boys home at a time and replace them with new ones so as to gradually develop a group culture. This was done by keeping the first group for a full six-weeks period and, after that, sending two boys home and replacing them with two new ones each week. It was simply amazing how quickly group values, group attitudes, group procedures, and group problem-solving ability developed.

Even with the turnover of two of the ten boys each week, it was possible to develop a group culture that did more than any two adults could ever do in handling negative behavior. I heard a counselor who had been in the program for over a year say to the supervisor, "If you had told me that we could get up and have breakfast without a problem, and sit in leisurely conversation thirty minutes after we finished, I would not have believed it. This is the best 'trip' I have ever been a part of.''

The program continued under this sort of organization until the Salesmanship Club decided to utilize the site in bringing to reality one of its long-cherished dreams—a permanent, fulltime, residential camp for girls.

GROUPWORK: AN EDUCATIONAL PROCESS

Responsibility promotes personal growth

Assuming that we have a suitable camp setting and a staff with sound psychological perspective, the program will flounder unless the counselors are able to utilize the group in the interest of each member. This requires that all members be involved in decisions affecting them—from the layout of the campsite to the food on the table; and they must share the responsibility for the success or failure of anything they undertake. Nowhere do boys have a fuller opportunity to make decisions and act on them than at camp. Without this freedom—even the freedom to fail—there is little opportunity for personal growth. It requires group discussion, the resolution of opposing views on the basis of as much information as they can obtain, and the evaluation of their success or failure.

An instance comes to mind when all the groups decided to build a one hundred twenty foot suspension bridge over a creek they had to cross each day. They planned to anchor the cables to an oak tree on each side, and attach the flooring to drop-cables that would give them a bridge five feet wide. There was a question as to whether the trees were strong enough to support the bridge but, after weighing the evidence, they decided to go ahead. For eight months they worked on the project, as time permitted, and completed a beautiful bridge; but when prolonged spring rains softened the ground, the red oak slowly bent its crown to earth and went to sleep. Not until then was it known that the tree was hollow near the ground, with a weakened root system. After a week or so of "mourning," the boys started another bridge, with a different design.

If the boys had not shared in the decisions along the way, they would not have had the heart to overcome their disappointment and start all over again with good spirit. If this process is short-circuited we are simply spinning our wheels.

Counselors are responsible for implementing the group process. It does not come naturally with kids, but it improves with practice. There is little basis for complaint by the boys when they have had a voice in deciding what they will do and how they will do it. We use this process in the chores around camp—the housekeeping things—and in what they will do today, next week or next month. They make their plans and set their priorities with minimum restrictions.

Rules and schedules

I doubt if there is a place in America where boys enjoy more freedom. We guard it jealously. Unless we do, restrictions, requirements and schedules envelop us like the arms of an octopus, crippling our efforts with time-binds and trivialities imposed for administrative reasons or supervisory convenience. Nothing will kill the initiative and spontaneity of a group quicker. We think long and hard before making a rule or a schedule at camp and never make one that we can possibly do without. They tend to creep in if there is a tendency to over-supervise, which means there is not sufficient trust in the boys or the counselors. No one can grow under these circumstances.

Leadership vs. management of a group

All of us agree that a good campsite is desirable. No individual or group can develop much pride on the basis of sloppy, irresponsible performance. All of us would work to achieve a neat and functional living area, but if a director or a groupwork supervisor wants to get the job done in a hurry, and it becomes an adult project, it will subvert the process and destroy the meaning it would otherwise achieve in the life of the boys.

I recall an instance of this when the campsite did need upgrading badly. It was pushed to completion by the subtle pressure and physical help of persons outside the group. The campsite was brought up to par. Everything was new except the dining tent. After a few weeks the group decided to replace it, and devised plans and worked on them with imagination and interest. Everything contributed toward a novel, unique, and functional dining tent. They drew plans of it and posted them on the bulletin board. They showed them to every visitor who came to their campsite with a pride we rarely saw exhibited; and finally they built it.

During the following few weeks I was in their campsite

many times, alone or with others, and it was interesting to see that this one tent was the emotional center of gravity for the whole group. It was the thing they mentioned first; it was the place they took visitors to see. They talked excitedly about how they planned it and why each detail was arranged as it was; but not once did I ever see them take a visitor to any other tent in the campsite. The reason was obvious.

I was in another campsite once which had been built up mostly by adults under the same procedure. I wanted to take a picture of their library and asked a nine year old boy to hold the door open so I could get a look at the books. When I took the picture we talked a minute, and I told him how nice the campsite looked, that I had never seen it look better in my life. He replied in a matter-of-fact way, "Yes, our campsite's all right, but our mental attitude isn't good."

No one can be indifferent to a campsite in disrepair, and all of us would want to see it upgraded; but the *process* by which it is done is the crucial thing. It is a question of leadership. If it is dominated by adults—even the counselors in the group—without the involvement of the members, the boys are reduced to laborers.

There is a vast difference between a group and an aggregation of ten boys. A group has common goals, mutual respect and concern for each other, and a plan of procedure. Without these there can be chaos.

Even if the feelings are positive between the group and its leaders, there is one other situation that may result in indifference to the use of the group. If the plans the boys make are not acted upon, if they are carelessly put together in a way that does not reflect genuine concern, or if they are unrealistic space fillers a counselor accepts with no serious intention of carrying out, it leads to certain failure. What is worse, if it happens often, it will bring contempt for the process—a dishonest approach through a spiritless and mechanical procedure that clearly reflects indifference to the welfare of the group.

If the process is not vital in one area, it will lose its effectiveness in others. If it is not successful in planning, it will not be effective in problem solving; and, furthermore, there would be no realistic basis for evaluations of group progress, which is necessarily based on what they set out to do.

Every effort is made to avoid the formation of subgroups that are prone to splinter off occasionally in a negative direction. A good leader will pull them in and hear them out in an effort to have their viewpoint considered. There is also a tendency for leadership to go to the more vocal members, and the counselor must be aware of each personality in the group and see that the timid, shy, insecure members are heard, too—that they are free from psychological or physical intimidation by the more aggressive members.

Discipline cannot exist in a group unless each member is free to voice his opinions with confidence that they will be considered. He is thus a part of all decisions affecting group life through a democratic process he regards as fair. When the program is planned and carried out in this way, it is a sound educational process.

If this process is not used *all* of the time, it will not work *any* of the time. If the counselor employs it in the solution of group problems but not in planning the camp layout, it will be regarded as a device he occasionally uses for his own convenience. This selective use of the process betrays our lack of faith and trust in the boys. They would regard it more as a technique we use than as a conviction we hold.

65

Suppose the group is planning to put poles across the trail to divert the water and prevent erosion. It will improve the morale of the group immensely if they know the purpose the poles will serve, the sizes required, and where they will get them. Such questions are discussed thoroughly before they begin. It gives meaning and purpose to the job.

Counselors develop skill and confidence

As a counselor gains experience in working with the group, he becomes more aware of little things that affect its operation. He will "feel the mood" of the group, and will detect little points of friction that would surely lead to trouble if he did not head them off. His efforts become more preventive. He develops wide-angle vision which enables him to assess the dynamics of the group more accurately. He develops confidence and self-assurance in working with the group. His energies go more toward preventing trouble than solving problems.

New counselors sometimes feel that if they spend too much time in group discussion they will "never get anything done." While it does take a new group some time to become skilled in the process, they do learn to use it effectively, and it turns out to be not only the most efficient way to do a job, but a way that bring the members into a more harmonious team. Actually, we do not have time *not* to do it.

Somewhere in the process a counselor lowers his voice, and the kids do, too. They communicate more easily. Sharp conflicts are reduced as they learn to function more cooperatively, as defiance and hositlty are reduced, as we uncross our wills and pursue common goals as friends.

We never reach a point where serious problems do not arise occasionally, but we have more skill in solving them and they are settled more quickly and with more satisfaction.

Boys will lose interest in group discussions quickly if they do not achieve positive results, or if they are unduly prolonged without progress toward a constructive settlement. In these situations they may resemble an endurance contest more than a problem-solving effort. This will occur if a counselor does not exercise leadership in bringing the discussion to a positive conclusion. This is a skill that counselors have to be taught, as few persons have it when they first come to camp. It is likely to be the missing ingredient when a group becomes negative and uncooperative.

This is apt to occur any time the method is used without the spirit or skill it presupposes. If the group is called together in anger, the chances of a positive outcome are sharply reduced. If a counselor uses some of the members to reinforce his own position against a minority point of view, or against a boy's hostile behavior, it will destory the process and alienate the members.

Overuse of the group process will kill its effectiveness, too. It can be used too often for minor friction that could best be handled with a band-aid: the situation is not serious enough to justify calling the group together, and too much time may be spent on trivialities, with no vital issue at stake. If the boys and the counselors become seriously divided, and there is antagonism between them, counselors may use the group negatively—almost as punishment.

All these things, of course, have implications for counselor training, and normally would not continue long. They cannot go unnoticed, as they will manifest themselves in all kinds of anti-social behavior.

Problem solving—an opportunity for growth

Each boy comes with at least one thing in common with all others—to solve a problem; but we do not deal with problems till they overtake us. We start out to meet our responsibilities and to have fun in doing it, and we deal with problems as they show up in a boy's behavior. In the early stages of group formation, mutual concern may be at a low ebb or even non-existent, and it is a primary responsibility of the counselors to develop among the members an attitude of helpfulness and goodwill. They learn this by example and through experience.

Our aim in discussing a problem caused by a boy is to help him find more appropriate ways of dealing with the situation. There is no blame, no punishment, only a recognition that his behavior was inappropriate and irresponsible. As we deal with one boy's problems, we help nine others.

Although we cannot *make* a boy do anything, we do not let his negative behavior go unnoticed. He cannot just walk away when he is finished. He has to take responsibility for his behavior, face the reaction of his buddies and the counselors; but all of them are his friends. He is not coerced. His dignity is not affronted. He is not mistreated. We demonstrate our friendship for him more convincingly in just such circumstances as these, perhaps, than in any other way.

This is no pleasant situation for a boy, for his peers face him squarely and forcefully. He is not shielded from *anything*, but he is supported by *everything*. I have not seen a boy who could withstand the consistent effort of the group to help him when it was done firmly and realistically, but with love.

We never ask a boy why he behaved as he did because, in the first place, he does not know, and it would not help if he did. We simply want him to see that his behavior was appropriate or inappropriate. There is no moralizing.

The counselor does not dominate the discussion, but he guides it in a way that elicits the honest feelings of all members. Through a counselor's own attitude and leadership the boys will begin to sense the spirit which we try to encourage in all our relationships. Experience will convince them of its vitality.

We do not regard problems as negative interruptions in our activities. Actually, they are opportunities for growth, for if they never surfaced, there would be little chance to help a boy in his interpersonal relationships. Many times the greatest satisfaction of the day comes from the successful conclusion of the group's effort to deal with ugly behavior that has completely wrecked the day's plans.

This is not wasted time. It is the only reason we are here. The program is consciously designed to provide time and flexibility to solve problems as they arise. Grudges, ill feelings, and resentment are heavy loads to carry and so we do not let them accumulate.

This is the general process used in considering any question before the group, whether of values, of program, of procedure or priorities. Our aim is to promote group participation in decisions affecting group life. It is done under conditions that allow each member to feel free in expressing his feelings or opinions. The counselor must lead these discussions. He raises questions and issues, facilitates discussion, summarizes it sometimes, and restates the conclusion that has been reached. It is a democratic procedure.

Group culture

Once a group is constituted, any change in its membership is gradual. A boy goes home and another takes his place. In this way the group structure is reasonably well maintained and we preserve the group culture which is the strongest and most positive influence in a boy's life at camp. Given a good group climate, and a program in keeping with the interests and needs of the boys, we have every reason to expect good results; but if either of these elements is absent, or impaired, it will adversely affect the morale of the group, which will lose cohesiveness and the ability to function well.

Even when appropriate psychological conditions exist in a group, it will still have problems of all kinds, but will be able to handle them in a way that makes them less likely to recur.

Application to the classroom

Perhaps the clearest result of our work with a boy is the total change in his attitude toward school, and his ability to function satisfactorily when he returns. When a change of this magnitude occurs, when a boy who has hated school for years returns eagerly and successfully, it is a major achievement, obvious to anyone.

The one thing that would be of immeasurable help to any teacher is the effective use of the class as a group. This idea would be nothing new to Education. Groupwork has a long history in both social work and education. In the former it is often employed as an adjunct to other therapeutic efforts, while schools have used the concept of grouping, and sometimes groupwork, as a device to improve effectiveness in teaching academic skills.

It is the process itself, however—the dynamics—that makes the difference. It is based upon psychological conditions, and teacher-pupil relationships, that have proved most favorable to learning.

A few years ago the Hogg Foundation for Mental Health, University of Texas, financed an experiment in which I worked part time during the Spring semester with the staff of Lamar School, in the Del Valle system, near Austin, to see if the techniques we used at Camp could be employed successfully in the classroom. Lamar School taught only students in Special Education.

It was decided I should work directly with the students and teachers in the usual classroom setting, around the opportunities and difficulties that normally present themselves in the day-to-day job. It was felt that any insights we arrived at, any beneficial result, would have more lasting effect, requiring no transfer from theory to practice.

There was a question as to what response we should expect from the various classes, but we worked with all of them just as we would work with any group, and they responded satisfactorily in class and on field trips.

Group process in the solution of problems took somewhat longer than with camp groups, but was no less effective. Some change in attitude was necessary for it even to begin, but it was increasingly productive. We used the group—the class—in setting norms for classroom behavior, for planning field trips, and for evaluations, using the same techniques we use with the more seriously handicapped boys at Camp. I am convinced they are as applicable in one place as another, though I should never have known this for sure without the excellent opportunity this experience afforded. Staff evaluation of the results was uniformly positive.

This leads me to say that I believe one of the most neglected areas of teacher training is in the use of the class as a group. The students can do more to set reasonable limits on classroom behavior, and to help establish levels of performance in all areas, than we can achieve in any other way I know; and the trust we thus place in them, and the relationship this implies, does much to establish an emotional climate most favorable for teaching and for over-all personal growth.

COUNSELOR TRAINING

Vital role of the counselor

It is obvious that the success or failure of our work with a boy depends on the counselor. A boy is intimately and continuously associated with his two counselors from the time he comes to camp until he leaves. The help we provide a boy is directly related to the counselor's effectiveness on the job.

We try to employ mature persons of good character who are interested in working with youth. If we are successful, the job itself will bring the counselor's moral and religious values into sharper focus. It is almost inevitable. One cannot do this job satisfactorily in neutral nor can he help boys effectively unless his own values are sound. These things become evident fairly soon.

Generalized goodwill, however, will not do the job. Our work must be underpinned with professional techniques that come from an understanding of child growth and development, from psychology, from mental health and from other professional disciplines. We have not labeled our work in these terms, but they are implicit in all we do. Kids can understand concern and helpfulness and decency, but they strangle on words that are not matched by action. We need people with love in their hearts, but also in their hands, their feet and their head. Such people declare their faith in action more than in words.

This is the only level on which we can reach kids when they first come to our attention. Love has to be implemented in concrete and specific ways in order to be effective. Through guided living experiences we try to help boys develop self-responsibility. Our aim is not some spectacular achievement—though this may occur—but learning to meet our ordinary life responsibilities well. This brings the deepest satisfaction a boy experiences.

The counselor has a big job, but if he is the kind of person we seek—positive, confident, optimistic—he will see first the tremendous opportunity it offers: an environment that stimulates the interest and curiosity of every boy, the freedom to plan and carry out their own small-group activities with minimum restrictions, with assurance that help is available immediately if needed.

We train a counselor exactly as we do a boy: we help him at the point he cannot function satisfactorily. Our attitude in working with him is the same as it is with the boys. We have confidence in his desire and ability to do the job well, and we help him when he cannot. Just as there is a group culture in each small campsite, there is also a staff culture that manifests itself in the willingness and desire to help each other in any way we can.

There are dozens of physical skills related to camping that can be taught in a relatively short time, but they must be taught. It is no longer a safe assumption that a twenty-five year old man can use the axe well, or saw a log in two, or dig a post hole, or lash a timber. He may encounter for the first time the need for dozens of skills that are commonplace in the life of the group.

More important is his attitude, his faith in people, his interest and persistence in helping them, his ability to stimulate interest, enthusiasm and cooperation. We expect a full effort but not full success. He must be free to experience group failure without a feeling of personal inadequacy. He must have a safety value, must know when to call for reinforcement if the group falls apart or gets out of hand; and he must be helped to see this failure of the group to function well, not just as a failure, but as an opportunity to learn and grow.

A major task of a counselor is to achieve enough understanding and maturity to see a boy's anti-social behavior as an effort to meet a life situation, struggling against odds he does not know how to cope with satisfactorily. It is helpful if, when a boy becomes aggressive or violent, the counselor can still see him as a good kid out of control—not as a bad kid. This is probably the hardest thing a new counselor has to do. When he has dealt with the boy patiently, honestly, fairly, and the boy's hostility and defiance still continue, it is easy to lose perspective and react in ways that make matters worse.

Groupwork skills

A counselor usually requires more help in groupwork than anything else. He has a group of ten boys with varying degrees of antisocial attitudes and behavior. There are no fences, no guards, nothing to keep a boy from walking off if he chooses to do so. The only control a counselor has over any boy is through the relationship that exists between them.

He is responsible for helping the group develop its own goals and purposes through a democratic process that allows for free expression by each member, and for promoting the group organization necessary to accomplish them. Few schools, if any, train a person for this sort of undertaking, and we have never found any one who was equipped to do the job when he came. Much of the director's time, and all of the groupwork supervisor's, is spent in teaching the counselors the various skills they need in order to do the job well.

Some counselors feel that boys are reached best through a bold and active program. They are action-oriented and, through their own enthusiasm, can provide leadership and momentum for a while. Other counselors are inclined to be too passive or analytical. They spend too much time in figuring out why a boy behaves as he does, as though it mattered, and the group falls apart as they ponder it; and there are all gradations in between. The groupwork supervisor has to be sufficiently sensitive to know when a group needs help, even if it is not requested.

New counselors often lack the skill to lead group discussions to a fruitful conclusion. They lack the experience to guide them effectively. Everyone feels free to talk, but the discussion does not get anywhere. No decisions are reached; or perhaps the more aggressive, vocal boys may carry their point if the timid boys do not feel free to express their feelings. It is difficult to teach these skills in the abstract, and the only successful way we have found is for the groupwork supervisor, or another person skilled in the process, to involve himself in these discussions and teach by example. They can be analyzed later. We can always do this without intruding because we are so closely related that none of us is really "outside" the group in spirit or purpose, and the boys know this.

Knowing a boy's strengths

Nothing is more important in developing a sound group process, or in a boy's over-all growth, than the counselor's demonstrated interest in each member. For the group process to be effective he must know intimately their problems and difficulties but, even more important, he must know their strengths. This is what we build on. The positive factors in a boy's personality are so much greater than his liabilities that it immediately gives us a basis for hope; and as we employ his strengths in the interest of the group, his satisfaction is increased and his negative behavior is correspondingly reduced. We use the *group* to deal with the *individual* more effectively.

A simple, but often overlooked way of letting a boy know we are interested in him, is simply by taking the natural opportunities that come now and then to discuss with him the progress he is making, the skills he has acquired, the positive attitudes he has exhibited.

We have to be absolutely honest about this and never go beyond what the facts warrant. We cannot encourage a person on the basis of empty praise. Only responsible performance affords him any basis for self-respect; but it helps a boy to know that we are sufficiently aware of him, as an individual, to observe the small but positive changes that he is gradually making. He will know beyond any doubt that the counselor is doing this because of his interest in him. There is no problem to be solved; the mood of the group is good; the "goose hangs high"; only the counselor's concern for the boy leads him to do it. It

77

builds a boy's sense of self-worth, and improves his relationship with the counselor. Over a period of time it will help the boy to participate more freely and constructively as a member of the group.

The growth of a counselor, in one sense, is from his concern with "big" things to "little" things, from the panorama to the detail, from the general to the specific. He has less need to seek adventure in long trips and high mountains when he learns to find it in his own back yard. I think we have erred in not emphasizing sufficiently the priceless opportunities they have right at hand. If we know what is the most important next step in each boy's growth, we will be able to achieve it wherever we are.

Discipline through goals—purposes

Control and discipline in a group are related directly and primarily to a counselor's understanding of the group process. It resides in the individual and group goals which the boys set for themselves. That is where it ought to be. It is the only way we can justify the freedom groups have to operate pretty much on their own; and without such freedom the opportunities for growth would be sharply reduced.

We cannot build control into physical structures, only function. Nominal supervision in the campsite is sometimes made easier by the arrangement of the sleeping shelters, but if a boy really wants to leave camp he will not use the front entrance.

To take a recent example, the boys in one group were making too much noise at the camp store when they came to get their food. It had become habitual. In order to quiet their unruly behavior, someone suggested that books be placed down there with the thought that the boys might read them instead of raising hell. If this approach were followed, we would need a lot of books in a lot of places. We simply cannot put out the thousand little fires that are symptomatic of an irresponsible or unskilled counselor. The behavior in question was not defiant or hostile, just a case of "situational itch" which a more experienced counselor could handle in a dozen different ways.

I emphasize the point that when groups are not operating well it has implications for counselor training and not for the hiring of additional staff or the formulation of more rules. If we get hemmed in by rules, schedules, and "no-no's," it will stifle the most priceless asset we have—the freedom and responsibility of groups to act in relation to their own needs—for freedom and responsibility cannot be separated.

Values—attitudes—academics

Since groups arrive at their own goals, they understand not only what they are going to do but how they are going to do it, and why. If this process is consistently maintained, they cannot avoid a broad education. Conventional academic skills are required all the time. New counselors sometimes wonder how they can get around to education, how they will find time for it, but actually, if the group is functioning well it is in everything they do, and they have all the time there is.

Physical skills are usually taught when they are needed, as a counselor would naturally have an opportunity to teach a boy how to cut wood when they need a fire. Academically, he might help a boy with his spelling when he writes a letter to his mother. I have never seen boys more thrilled or excited than when they achieve some academic skill that they should have learned two or three years before but did not. They are simply elated. Few things are more rewarding to a boy than overcoming educational deficits that may have snowballed into academic failure. When any counselor sees the meaning of this kind of disability in a boy, he will find a dozen ways to overcome it.

With attitudes, it is something else. A group's values, attitudes, and the norms of behavior they expect of themselves, emerge out of their experience and are refined through group discussion. Each group has a nightly evaluation called the pow-wow, the last thing before they go to bed, and its purpose is to take a look at the day and evaluate their performance. Their plans for the day give them a background against which to measure their efforts. Did they get done what they had planned? They try to recognize anything that might have kept them from it or, on the other hand, anything that promoted unusual group success. They profit from the insights they gain in this way.

It is also in the pow-wow where the boys set their own norms of behavior; for instance, if the group has been unusually loud in the dining room of late, a counselor or boy may casually ask, "How do you think we are doing in the dining room these days?" If there is general agreement, as there usually is, that they have been a little out of bounds, the counselor may ask, "What do you think we need to do about it?" In the discussion that follows, the group decides the level of conduct they will expect of themselves. It is usually sufficient. If infractions occur the next day, or later, the counselor simply needs to remind them, as it is not usually intentional.

The same process is used in any other area. If the

counselor feels that there is too much profanity in their conversation, he may follow the same pattern; or, if they are having a hard time getting to breakfast on time, the group may decide to get up fifteen minutes earlier. It is easy to get adherence to agreements arrived at in this way, whereas it would be impossible otherwise.

We sometimes make the mistake of thinking that education is something kids would like to avoid, but actually a boy feels miserable when he is significantly behind academically, and would work his heart out to catch up if he had any hope of success. He verifies this through the questions he asks and the curiosity he exhibits.

Nothing depresses a group quicker than when they let their program become monotonous, with no new learning experiences. On the other hand, morale is never higher than when there is something novel in their day, or a new accomplishment. It does not have to be something big: a new twist to an old recipe, the "headlights" on a click beetle, or the first wild geese flying south. When counselors become aware of the meaning of such little things, there is simply no end to the opportunities that arise daily. Interest, morale, discipline and education are all involved.

Counselor support

No counselor will have smooth sailing right from the start. The boys will see to that. They will test him in ingenious ways that will tell them if he is interested, if he is fair, if he is firm, if he is honest, if he is responsible. But no matter how well he passes the test, he will still encounter problems now and then that he cannot handle.

The groupwork supervisor is available to help him through these situations and keep him from resorting to methods that deepen his conflict with the group. A new counselor can simply say, "I do not know what the procedure should be in this situation, but I am unwilling to go ahead as we are. This is not what I came here to do, and I do not want to be a part of it. I think we should get help." There is always someone in the group who can be depended on to take a message to the supervisor, and he is available on short notice.

It is no weakness to ask for help. In doing so a counselor does not compromise his own integrity, he does not affront the dignity of the boys, he does not resort to force, and when the problem is cleared there will be no battle scars between them, no ill feelings to overcome.

Usually a counselor is not faced with the responsibility of a group alone until he has had a little experience. He usually works with a counselor who has been in the program a while. But we make him aware that help is available if needed and urge him to stay within agency policy in working with the group so we can always support his position. If such help is not available over an extended period of time, a conscientious counselor will likely become frustrated and leave; and an immature counselor might settle with the boys on the basis of expediency and come to terms with them on a level of operation that we could not support. It would not be fair to the counselor or the boys to let this situation develop.

If a counselor gets the help he needs during the induction period, and his feeling of security develops, his emphasis in working with boys will be less on how to *control* them and more on how he can *help* them; and when a new boy comes to his group he is not seen as a troublesome boy who will foul up the program, but rather as a boy we can help.

Counselor is group leader

Only with experience does one achieve a balance in the use of the group as opposed to dealing with minor situations individually. A flare of tempers, an impulsive act with no steam behind it, can be handled individually then and there; but, if these are tendencies, it is something that may be dealt with more appropriately in the group in terms of attitude. Group destructive behavior, however, should be dealt with through the group as it arises. A counselor will know the psychological weight it carries and be governed accordingly.

It is a little like emphasizing the obvious to remind ourselves that group discussion requires a leader, and this responsibility cannot be abdicated with the thought that the group can settle their problems by themselves. I have seen this occur in a problem solving session in an institutional program where it amounted to little less than psychological torture for a member who came under massive attack from a hostile group. Any effort the girl made to defend herself was drowned out by a chorus of angry rejoinders—a perfect opportunity for scapegoating, or worse. The "leader" observed but did not participate in this chaotic free-for-all where growth was impossible and mere survival was difficult. Strangely enough, it was called group therapy. It is obvious that any unguided discussion by a group of maladjusted teen-agers can serve no therapeutic goal.

Kids have to be taught, and this would have been a good opportunity if the "leader" had led, and helped them to see whether the attitudes they were exhibiting would be helpful or harmful as a basis for group interaction.

It would be equally foolish to issue canvas, an axe, and a few hand tools to ten inexperienced, antisocial boys and expect them to develop decent camp shelters. No matter how much they wished to do it, they would first have to acquire a few skills, and this is the time to teach them. We cannot sit back and let cold or wet weather motivate them. Motivation is not their problem; it is skill they lack, and they cannot be· expected to get it from aloof or disinterested adults.

Counselor training is continuous

We do not expect an experienced counselor to take responsibility for training a new one who is assigned to his group, though he may be a tremendous help. Even good counselors sometimes have areas in which they are relatively weak. We prefer to assign a relief counselor to the group for brief periods so both counselors can share in the orientation, as it serves as a helpful review for the "old" counselor and promotes unity and teamwork in their approach to the job.

Periodic evaluations of a counselor's performance in all areas is a helpful counterpart to his day-to-day supervision. It brings into sharper focus the importance and relationship of all aspects of the job. Staff meetings are particularly useful in that they bring to bear the experience and viewpoints of each member on any area of our work. Their purpose and procedure is essentially the same as a group of boys and their leaders dealing with questions affecting their own operation. The ongoing help of the groupwork supervisor, as needed, is an indispensable part of giving implementation to the ideas and procedures agreed on in staff meetings.

Throughout our work with counselors our aim is to give them sufficient training in all areas of the job to permit them to operate with as much autonomy as possible. We teach counselors all we know about the layout and construction of the small group campsite, but it is up to them to build it. They are the ones to determine the number of sleeping shelters they will need and where they will be located, the shape of the dining tent, the type of cooking arrangement they prefer, the size of the craft tent and the location of the latrine. It would kill the spirit of a counselor, as well as the group, if we told them how to do these things.

Through our study of the weekly plans they submit, and our frequent trips through the campsite, we can keep sufficiently abreast of a group's progress to forestall any serious error of judgment. In such a case, we would mention it to the counselors and let them take it from there. Tight supervision is destructive of spirit and morale, and is not even effective in achieving group control. Neither our philosophy nor our organization would permit it. Counselors must act out of their own judgment, integrity and skill. The degree of freedom they enjoy is based on these considerations.

Rewards of the job

As a rule, we employ young men just out of college, or nearly so, who see the job as offering a good opportunity to perform a useful service. Compensation is adequate.

The job itself is not burdensome provided counselors

85

are helped to acquire the needed skills. More than all other factors combined, good training and supervision is the thing that keeps them on the job; and, the better they do the job, the easier and more effective their work becomes. There is no question of "burning out" when counselors have been well prepared for the job.

A natural corollary to good training is one's sense of personal and professional growth, which is obvious and deeply rewarding.

There is not much difference in the average length of stay at camp of boys and counselors. The best average we achieved for counselors was eighteen months, but this included a few who had been on the job much longer. We can manage very well on this basis.

It has been the consensus of counselors that they grew as much as the boys, and that they have left camp with many skills that are transferable to other professional disciplines.

The job is not feasible for married persons, but when counselors marry, they may accept a supervisory position on the staff, become directors of other camps patterned along the same lines, or go into related fields such as teaching, mental health, corrections, the ministry, child guidance, work with the physically handicapped or the mentally retarded; or functions in other areas of social work. Their growth is both personal and professional.

STARTING
A NEW CAMP

This chapter is included primarily for those who will be working with youth in camps.

Site

A good site is as important for camping as a choice location is for a merchant. I prefer a wooded tract, with hilly or rolling terrain, with water, and sufficiently isolated to avoid distractions; yet I know of successful camps that have operated for years without some of these features.

We camped for the first twelve years on a two-hundred-acre site just seven and one-half miles from downtown Dallas which, due to its unique location, afforded an unbelievable sense of isolation. There is a camp in Virginia on less than one hundred fifty acres, with no stream, lake, or pool, and not far from town; but it is surrounded on three sides by undeveloped property, and they have compensated for the lack of water in a way that has not impaired the program; but these are exceptions.

Some persons prefer a stream to a lake, and some prefer a three-acre lake to one of twenty acres, but we can get along without either. The one thing we can least do without is isolation.

Isolation is necessary for the small group campsites as well as for the tract as a whole. Each group needs to be out of the sight and hearing of others. This may be achieved by plant growth and topographical variations as much as by distance. Usually it is a combination of these.

In the South, with long growing seasons, the property can be improved enormously within just a few years by planting. The 115,000 seedlings we planted eighteen years ago now look like the Black Forest in places.

Surrounding property, and the likelihood of its development, is a factor that requires careful consideration. In these days of urban sprawl and industrial expansion, it is necessary to consider the likelihood of future encroachment, even when the site has several hundred acres well removed from towns or cities. In Texas and Florida, therapeutic camps have been located on land adjoining National Forests. The Forest Service has permitted construction of temporary facilities on forest land, and the use of the forest for hiking and exploration. This is in keeping with its policy of multiple use, and has the effect of reducing the amount of land that must be purchased. Obviously there are restrictions on timber cutting, but these are consonant with our own philosophy.

Pressley Ridge School, in Pittsburg, operates a therapeutic camp on a tract of seveal hundred acres it purchased outright, but which is further protected by a large and undeveloped State Park which it joins on the back side.

If such a natural buffer cannot be found, the amount of land purchased, or in some cases leased, must be increased to assure its adequacy. This will vary from one location to another.

We frequently hear our program referred to as "wilderness camping," but it is not. It is doubtful if we could even be licensed in a wilderness setting because ordinary prudence requires that we have ready access to medical care and hospital facilities. There is nothing more rewarding than an ocassional stint in the wilderness, but it would not be a preferred residential campsite.

The availability of supplies and equipment is a factor, as well as the contact of boys with their families from time to time. Some camps serve large areas, and parents do not ordinarily visit camp; but our own program serves youth from Dallas County only, and we have frequent contact at camp with their families—and persons from the agencies that refer them—during the intake process and in subsequent evaluations of a boy's progress.

Therapeutic camping does not require elaborate site development and we use the fewest trails, the fewest roads, and the fewest buildings possible. Service buildings are grouped in one area so they will be functionally related and served by one road, if possible. This helps preserve, intact, the rest of the site for the use of the campers.

Buildings and other facilities

Utilities, sanitation facilities and health requirements are different for each state and locality, and new camps will be governed by regulations that apply in each area.

Permanent structures include a dining room-kitchen, warehouse, bath house, office, and a residence for the director and the groupwork supervisor. We did not start with these in the beginning, because our program was experimental then. We used a tent for an office, and a war-surplus navy hospital tent for a dining room. It was a satisfactory arrangement for the first year or more, and the buildings were added later.

Many different arrangements for office space have proved satisfactory. It depends to some extent on how the program is organized, where the bills are paid, the records kept, location of the Intake Office, and other things. With the heavy use of our office for family conferences, staff meetings, and day-to-day administration, we prefer a separate location where truck deliveries, dishwashing, mealtime preparation, or heavy traffic are not an intrusion.

When we moved to our present site, the bathhouse and warehouse were the only buildings we had for the first eight months, and everyone lived in tents through the wettest Spring in Texas history; but we had an experienced staff and experienced campers who knew how to cope with the circumstances without discomfort or frustration.

Function determines structure, so it is essential in site development and building design that the function of each facility, and its relation to all others, be considered in detail. I have seen several satisfactory designs for providing the essential services, each one being influenced by topographical features or variations in program.

Buildings should be simple and functional, in keeping with camp philosophy and purpose. They should reflect the same values as the camp itself. Though providing comfort and efficiency, they should intrude as little as possible on the simplicity of camp life, and create no psychological shock as one moves from the campsite to the central buildings.

It is easy to overbuild and, as a rule of thumb, it is not good to build anything we can do without. The program operates best when it is lean and a little hungry, whether in buildings, equipment or personnel. We can easily escalate our requirements until we cannot take a cross-country hike, for example, without an aluminum packframe for each boy, costing fifty or seventy-five dollars. On the other hand, we can build our own, out of material on the campsite, that serve us well. Affluence can be a problem as well as poverty. We try to teach kids to live responsibly in the outdoors with simple and inexpensive equipment, items which a self-reliant boy from a poor neighborhood could fashion with a pocket knife, binder twine, or other inexpensive tools and materials.

Economy and simplicity

One of our long-standing aims is to keep the program vital, simple, and as economical as possible. To do this, it is necessary to minimize the capital investment and emphasize the quality and training of staff. It is the best way we have found to help the boys, and it results in a cost-effectiveness ratio that communities can afford. Although basic facilities are absolutely essential, *people* make the difference. Simplicity is the essence of our program but, for various reasons, it is one of the hardest things to maintain.

These considerations are in keeping with our emphasis on conservation—the wise use of our resources—including money.

A new program needs the assurance of dependable funding for the level of operation that is anticipated. A director cannot function effectively if he must spend his time seeking financial support. Few things threaten the success of a program as much as inadequate and uncertain financing.

Staff

Staff should be selected who have had training or experience in this or related fields of work. No matter how well this is done, it will be necessary to provide a month or so of training before the program begins.

No one comes equipped to handle all aspects of the work, and most of the training must be provided on the job. A good opportunity is presented in building the campsite facilities for the first group. This must be done before the campers arrive so they will have a suitable place to live; and it gives the staff an opportunity to work together in the very same way they will be teaching the campers, doing the same things. Perhaps as important as anything else, the staff comes to know each other and learns to work together effectively.

Interspersed in this process are discussions of the camp's philosophy and ways of implementing it in daily life. We teach counselors exactly as they will teach the boys.

We serve fifty boys, and our staff over the years has consisted of a director, secretary, groupwork supervisor, a roving counselor, a cook and cook's helper, service manager, maintenance man, and two counselors for each group of boys. This does not include the staff of the Intake Office in Dallas.

The work of the service-maintenance staff varies somewhat depending on such things, for example, as whether the roads are maintained by the camp staff, whether the laundry is done commercially or at camp, and the skill of the maintenance man in the repair of such diverse things as camp vehicles, water lines, sewage lines, electrical services, buildings, and so on.

The counseling staff consists of two counselors for each group of ten boys, and a "roving" counselor to fill in, if necessary, in the case of illness, vacations, or otherwise as needed; and a groupwork supervisor. This has proved adequate.

Staff-camper ratio

We sought and obtained from the licensing agency a waiver of the requirement that there be a minimum of one person on duty at all times for each six boys. Our thirty years of successful experience was taken into consideration.

The addition of a third counselor to a group complicates group functioning in several ways. First, it requires fifty percent more time in recruiting, training and supervising the extra staff that would be needed. Second, it requires more time in coordinating the work in each group with three counselors involved. It takes longer for them to reach a decision, to formulate group plans, and to move into action. It is harder for them to even get together for planning purposes. Third, though it is harder to explain than to observe, there is an obvious loss of pride that a counselor has in his group, due, I think, to the fact that the responsibility is too diffused. It is harder for a counselor to feel that the group's success or failure is due to his own efforts.

These are things we have observed from experience, for at one time it was tried. It was the consensus of everyone—especially the counselors—that groups functioned better with only two leaders. The group values, the group culture, which counselors are able to induce is more influential in group control than anything we have discovered. Without this, three counselors—or even six—would be helpless and hopeless in an open environment such as camp.

How many to serve

We have found it best to start a new camp with one group and confine our efforts to it until it is functioning smoothly. Other groups can be added, one at a time, as staff and experience permit. It is a mistake to expand the program too fast. We need to become sound in the operation of the first group before adding the second. This gives the staff time to develop skills and techniques in all aspects of our work, and enables us to move with confidence and self-assurance as the program is gradually enlarged.

From the standpoint of cost and efficiency we find fifty is the maximum number we can serve in a camp. For a short period we exceeded that number. It was found, however, that service units have to be doubled in some areas, that there was less time for the close and continuing work with the counselors, and that our intimate awareness of each boy's individual circumstances was more difficult to maintain.

Experience has shown that, over an extended period of time, we can actually help more boys if we limit the number we serve at a time, and serve them well.